Assessment Book

PEARSON
Scott Foresman

Editorial Offices: Glenview, Illinois • Parsippany, New Jersey • New York, New York
Sales Offices: Parsippany, New Jersey • Duluth, Georgia • Glenview, Illinois
Coppell, Texas • Ontario, California

www.sfsocialstudies.com

Program Authors

Dr. Candy Dawson Boyd
Professor, School of Education
Director of Reading Programs
St. Mary's College
Moraga, California

Dr. Geneva Gay
Professor of Education
University of Washington
Seattle, Washington

Rita Geiger
Director of Social Studies and
  Foreign Languages
Norman Public Schools
Norman, Oklahoma

Dr. James B. Kracht
Associate Dean for
  Undergraduate Programs
  and Teacher Education
College of Education
Texas A & M University
College Station, Texas

Dr. Valerie Ooka Pang
Professor of Teacher Education
San Diego State University
San Diego, California

Dr. C. Frederick Risinger
Director, Professional
  Development and Social
  Studies Education
Indiana University
Bloomington, Indiana

Sara Miranda Sanchez
Elementary and Early
  Childhood Curriculum
  Coordinator
Albuquerque Public Schools
Albuquerque, New Mexico

Contributing Authors

Dr. Carol Berkin
Professor of History
Baruch College and the
  Graduate Center
The City University of New York
New York, New York

Lee A. Chase
Staff Development Specialist
Chesterfield County
  Public Schools
Chesterfield County, Virginia

Dr. Jim Cummins
Professor of Curriculum
Ontario Institute for Studies
  in Education
University of Toronto
Toronto, Canada

Dr. Allen D. Glenn
Professor and Dean Emeritus
College of Education
Curriculum and Instruction
University of Washington
Seattle, Washington

Dr. Carole L. Hahn
Professor, Educational Studies
Emory University
Atlanta, Georgia

Dr. M. Gail Hickey
Professor of Education
Indiana University-Purdue
  University
Ft. Wayne, Indiana

Dr. Bonnie Meszaros
Associate Director
Center for Economic Education
  and Entrepreneurship
University of Delaware
Newark, Delaware

ISBN 0-328-03090-2

Copyright © Pearson Education, Inc.
All Rights Reserved. Printed in the United States of America. The blackline masters in this publication are designed for use with appropriate equipment to reproduce copies for classroom use only. Scott Foresman grants permission to classroom teachers to reproduce from these masters.

9 10-V016-11 10 09 08

Contents

Unit 1: Our Big Book of Who We Are
Vocabulary Assessment 1
Target Reading Skill Assessment 2
Content Assessment 3–4

Unit 2: Our Big Book of Communities
Vocabulary Assessment 5
Target Reading Skill Assessment 6
Content Assessment 7–8

Unit 3: Our Big Book of Work
Vocabulary Assessment 9
Target Reading Skill Assessment 10
Content Assessment 11–12

Unit 4: Our Big Book of the Earth
Vocabulary Assessment 13
Target Reading Skill Assessment 14
Content Assessment 15–16

Unit 5: Our Big Book of the U.S.A.
Vocabulary Assessment 17
Target Reading Skill Assessment 18
Content Assessment 19–20

Unit 6: Our Big Book of Family Stories
Vocabulary Assessment 21
Target Reading Skill Assessment 22
Content Assessment 23–24

Answer Key 25–30

To the Teacher

Every teacher collects information (assesses) while teaching. Teachers listen to children's responses, observe their performance during activities, note cooperation and interaction among children, and identify children who are not involved in the learning process. Much of this assessment happens informally. This informal assessment data, plus data from more formal assessments, are used to modify instruction and improve learning.

One way to evaluate the success of your social studies instruction lies in using the assessment options provided in **Scott Foresman** *Social Studies*. These options will help you measure children's progress toward social studies instructional goals.

The assessment tools provided with **Scott Foresman** *Social Studies* can

- help you determine which children need more help and where classroom instruction needs to be reinforced, reviewed, or expanded.
- help you evaluate how well children comprehend, communicate, and apply what they have learned.

Scott Foresman *Social Studies* provides a comprehensive assessment package as shown below.

Assessment Options Available in Scott Foresman *Social Studies*

Formal Assessments	✓ Unit Review ✓ Unit Tests, Assessment Book
Informal Assessments	✓ Teacher's Edition Questions ✓ Close and Assess
Portfolio Assessments	✓ Portfolio Assessment ✓ Leveled Practice ✓ Workbook Pages ✓ Unit Review ✓ Curriculum Connection
Performance Assessments	✓ Hands-on Unit Project ✓ Unit Review ✓ Scoring Guides

Overview of Assessment Book

Big Book Assessments

The Unit Assessments are a tool to evaluate children's understanding of social studies concepts and their ability to apply and analyze the concepts. There is a four-page reproducible assessment for each unit.

Children are asked to draw or color an answer, write an answer, match items, and choose a correct answer from a series of possible responses.

At the back of the Assessment Book, there is an answer key for each Unit Assessment.

Part 1: Vocabulary
The one-page vocabulary assessment evaluates children's knowledge of and ability to apply the oral vocabulary introduced in each unit.

Part 2: Reading Social Studies
The one-page reading assessment evaluates children's knowledge of and ability to apply the target reading skill introduced in each unit.

Part 3: Content
The two-page content assessment evaluates children's knowledge of and ability to answer the unit question. The activities are designed to cover levels of thinking from knowledge to comprehension and application.

Unit Tests: Objectives Assessed

Unit 1 Test	• Determine the meaning of words. • Use picture clues to aid comprehension. • Identify ways in which people are alike and different. • Identify and follow school rules to insure order and safety. • Participate constructively in school and classroom activities.
Unit 2 Test	• Determine the meaning of words. • Classify and categorize pictures. • Identify common signs and symbols. • Describe people and places in the community. • Summarize jobs performed by community workers.
Unit 3 Test	• Determine the meaning of words. • Compare and contrast pictures. • Identify different kinds of jobs. • Match simple descriptions of the work that people do with the names of those jobs.

Unit 4 Test	• Determine the meaning of words. • Recognize cause and effect. • Describe common characteristics of forests. • Describe common characteristics of plains. • Describe common characteristics of mountains. • Describe common characteristics of oceans.
Unit 5 Test	• Determine the meaning of words. • Identify and order events that take place in a sequence. • Compare people, objects, and events of today and long ago. • Identify examples of past events. • Recognize the American flag.
Unit 6 Test	• Determine the meaning of words. • Recall a familiar story, activity, or event and retell it. • Distinguish likenesses and differences among individuals and families. • Give examples of how families cooperate and work together. • Describe aspects of families.

NOTES

Name _____

Big Book 1
Assessment

Vocabulary

✏️ Circle.

Directions: (Row 1) Look at the pictures. Use a blue crayon to circle the picture of a family. (Row 2) Look at the pictures. Use a red crayon to circle the picture of an apartment building. Use a blue crayon to circle the picture of a townhouse. (Row 3) Look at the pictures. Use a blue crayon to circle the picture of the nurse. Use a red crayon to circle the picture of the teacher.

Assessment Book Unit 1 Test

Big Book 1

Name _____

Big Book 1 Assessment

Reading Social Studies
Use Illustrations

Color.

Directions: (Top) Color the picture clues that tell you it is cold outside. (Bottom) Color the picture clues that tell you it is hot outside.

2 Big Book 1

Assessment Book Unit 1 Test

Name _____

Big Book 1 Assessment

How are people alike and different?

✏️ Color.

Directions: (Top) Look at the picture to see how these girls are different. Color the things that are different about the girls. (Bottom) Look at the picture to see how these boys are alike. Color the things that are alike about the boys.

Assessment Book Unit 1 Test

Big Book 1

Name _____

Big Book 1 Assessment

How are people alike and different?

🖊 Circle.   🖍 Draw.

Directions: Use a red crayon to circle the children who are not following good rules for being in a line. Use a blue crayon to circle the child who is trying to help. Draw yourself in the picture. Share your picture with a partner to tell how the children are alike and different.

Big Book 1

Assessment Book Unit 1 Test

Name _____

Big Book 2
Assessment

Vocabulary

Color.

Directions: (Row 1) Look at the pictures. Color the firefighter red. Color the police officer blue. Color the chef green. (Row 2) Look at the pictures. Color the home in the suburbs blue. Color the home in the country green. Color the home in the city red.

Assessment Book Unit 2 Test

Big Book 2 5

Name _____

Big Book 2 Assessment

Reading Social Studies
Classify/Categorize

✂ Cut.

Inside

Outside

Directions: Look at the toys. Cut out the pictures of the toys. Paste the pictures in the spaces to show inside toys and outside toys.

6 Big Book 2

Assessment Book Unit 2 Test

Name _____

Big Book 2 Assessment

What is a community?

✏️ Circle.

✏️ Draw.

Directions: (Top) Look at this community. Circle the signs you see in the community. (Bottom) Draw a picture of a sign you see in your community.

Assessment Book Unit 2 Test   Big Book 2   **7**

Name _____

Big Book 2 Assessment

What is a community?

✏️ Circle.

✏️ Draw.

Directions: (Row 1) Look at the pictures. Circle the community workers who help keep people safe. (Row 2) Look at the pictures. Circle the picture that most looks like the community where you live. (Bottom) Draw a picture to show something you like about your community.

Big Book 2

Assessment Book Unit 2 Test

Name _____

Big Book 3
Assessment

Vocabulary

✏ Circle.

Directions: (Top) Look at the pictures. Use a red crayon to circle the firefighter. Use a blue crayon to circle the chef. Use a green crayon to circle the photographer. (Bottom) Look at the picture. Use a red crayon to circle the food. Use a blue crayon to circle the clothing. Use a green crayon to circle the shelter.

Assessment Book Unit 3 Test

Big Book 3 9

Name _____

**Big Book 3
Assessment**

Reading Social Studies
Compare and Contrast

Color.

Directions: Look at the two pictures. Think about how the pictures are alike and different. Color the things that are alike.

10 Big Book 3

Assessment Book Unit 3 Test

Name _____

Big Book 3 Assessment

What kinds of work do people do?

✏️ Color.

Directions: Look at the picture. Color the workers in the picture.

Assessment Book Unit 3 Test

Big Book 3 **11**

Name _____

Big Book 3 Assessment

What kinds of work do people do?

✏️ Draw.

Directions: Draw a picture to show a worker you know. Show what kind of work the person does.

Big Book 3

Assessment Book Unit 3 Test

Name _____

Big Book 4
Assessment

Vocabulary

✏ Circle.

Directions: (Top) Look at the pictures. Use a green crayon to circle the summer picture. Use a blue crayon to circle the winter picture. Use a red crayon to circle the fall picture. (Bottom) Look at the pictures. Use a green crayon to circle the forest picture. Use a blue crayon to circle the plains picture. Use a red crayon to circle the mountain picture.

Assessment Book Unit 4 Test   Big Book 4   13

Name _____

Big Book 4 Assessment

Reading Social Studies
Cause and Effect

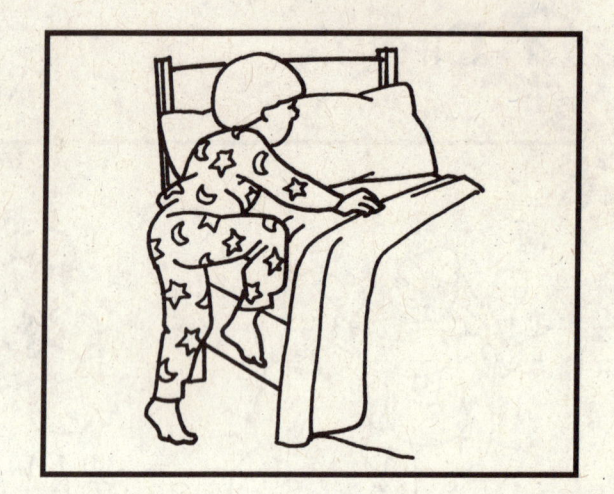

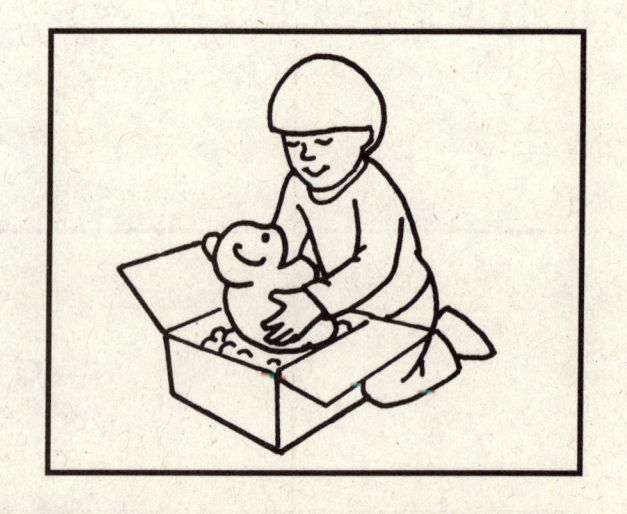

✏️ Draw.   🖍️ Color.

Directions: Look at each picture. Draw a line from the first picture in each row to the picture that shows what happened. Color each picture that shows what happened.

14 Big Book 4

Assessment Book Unit 4 Test

Name _____

**Big Book 4
Assessment**

What does our Earth look like?

✏️ Draw.

Forest

Plain

Directions: (Top) Draw a picture to show a forest and an animal that might live there. (Bottom) Draw a picture to show a plain and an animal that might live there.

Assessment Book Unit 4 Test

Name _____

**Big Book 4
Assessment**

What does our Earth look like?

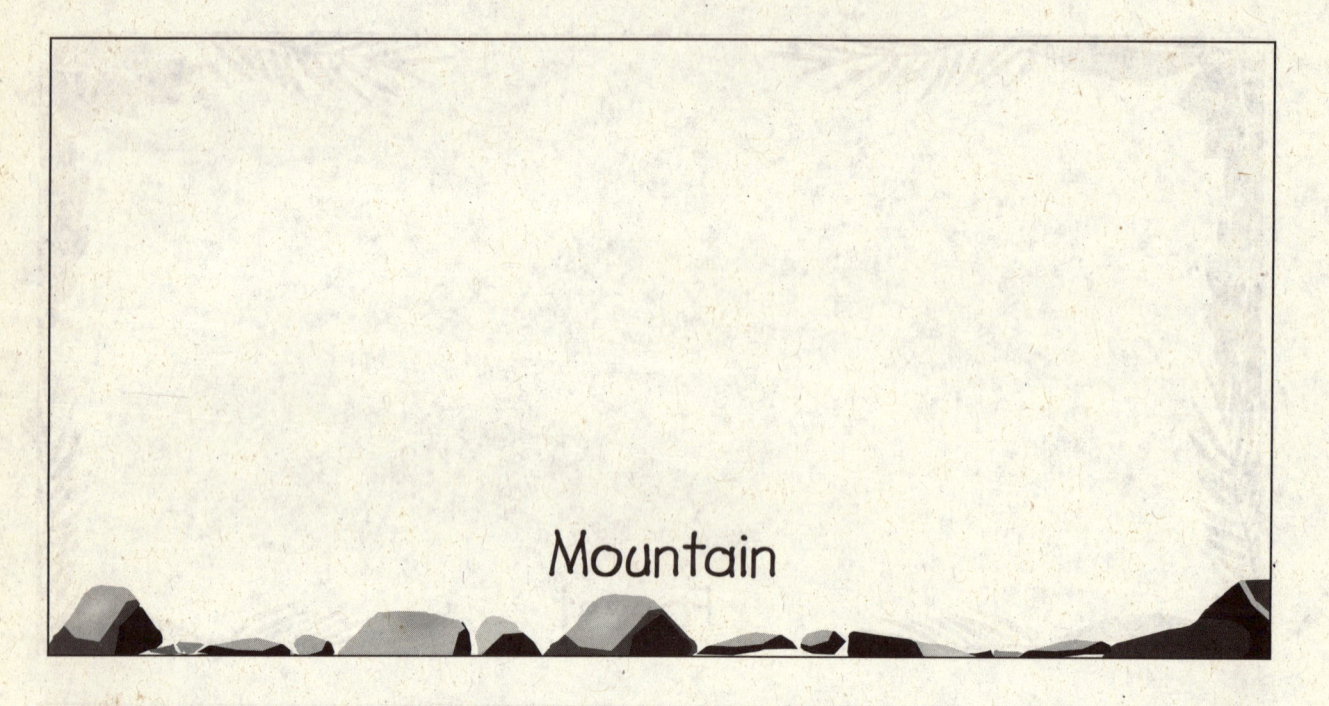

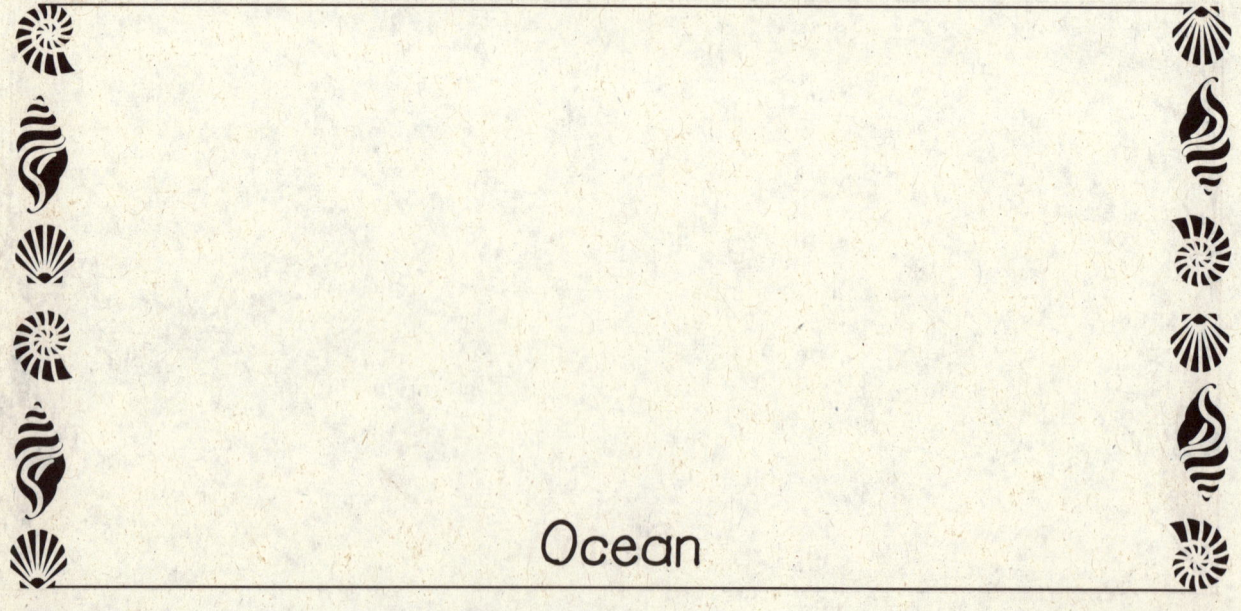

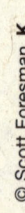

✎ Draw.

Mountain

Ocean

Directions: (Top) Draw a picture to show a mountain and an animal that might live there. (Bottom) Draw a picture to show an ocean and an animal that might live there.

Big Book 4

Assessment Book Unit 4 Test

Name _____

Big Book 5
Assessment

Vocabulary

✏ Circle.

Directions: (Row 1) Look at the pictures. Use a blue crayon to circle the Statue of Liberty. Use a red crayon to circle the American flag. (Row 2) Look at the pictures. Use a blue crayon to circle Pocahontas. Use a red crayon to circle George Washington. (Row 3) Look at the pictures. Use a blue crayon to circle the train. Use a red crayon to circle the covered wagon.

Assessment Book Unit 5 Test

Big Book 5 **17**

Name _____

Big Book 5 Assessment

Reading Social Studies
Sequence

✏️ Write.   🖍️ Color.

Directions: Look at the pictures. Think about what happens first, next, and last. Write *1*, *2*, and *3* to show what happens first, next, and last. Then color the pictures.

18 Big Book 5   Assessment Book Unit 5 Test

Name _____

Big Book 5 Assessment

How has our country changed?

✏️ Circle.   🖍️ Color.

Now Then	Now Then

Now Then	Now Then

Directions: Look at the pictures. Circle *Now* if the picture shows what our country is like today. Circle *Then* if the picture shows what our country was like long ago. Color the pictures.

Assessment Book Unit 5 Test

Name _____

Big Book 5 Assessment

How has our country changed?

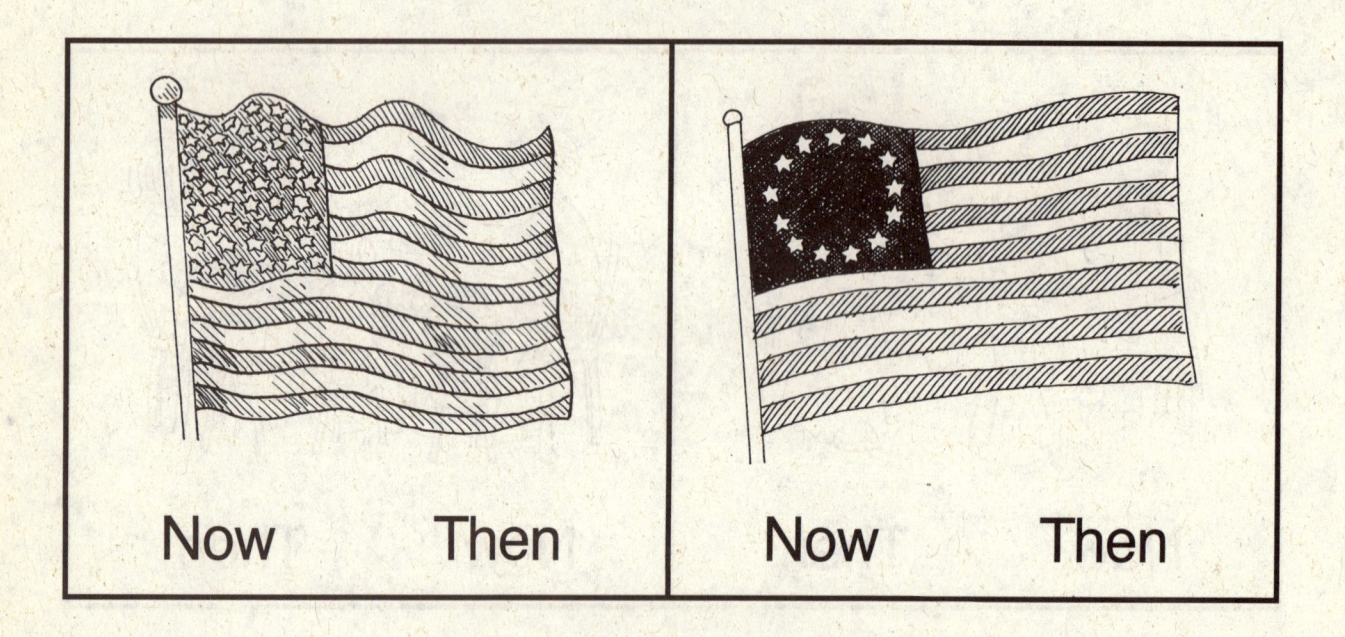

🖉 Circle.   🖍 Color.

| Now   Then | Now   Then |
| Now   Then | Now   Then |

🍎 **Directions:** Look at the pictures. Circle *Now* if the picture shows what our country is like today. Circle *Then* if the picture shows what our country was like long ago. Color the pictures.

20 Big Book 5   Assessment Book Unit 5 Test

Name _____

Big Book 6
Assessment

Vocabulary

✏ Circle.

Directions: (Row 1) Look at the pictures. Use a blue crayon to circle one reason a family might celebrate. Use a red crayon to circle one way a family might play together. (Row 2) Look at the pictures. Use a blue crayon to circle one way a family might work together. Use a red crayon to circle something made with a family recipe.

Assessment Book Unit 6 Test

Big Book 6   **21**

Name _____

Big Book 6 Assessment

Reading Social Studies
Recall and Retell

Draw.

Directions: Think about an activity the class has done together. Draw a picture to recall the activity. Use your picture to retell the activity to the class.

Big Book 6

Assessment Book Unit 6 Test

Name _____

Big Book 6 Assessment

What is special about families?

✏️ Color.

[Picture: Families work together.]

✏️ Draw.

My family works together.

Directions: (Top) Color the picture of the family working together. (Bottom) Draw a picture to show a way your family works together. Then tell how the family pictures are alike and different.

Assessment Book Unit 6 Test

Name _____

Big Book 6 Assessment

What is special about families?

✏️ Color.

Families have fun together.

✏️ Draw

My family has fun together.

Directions: (Top) Color the picture of the family having fun together. (Bottom) Draw a picture to show a way your family has fun together. Then tell how the family pictures are alike and different.

Big Book 6

Assessment Book Unit 6 Test

© Scott Foresman K

Vocabulary

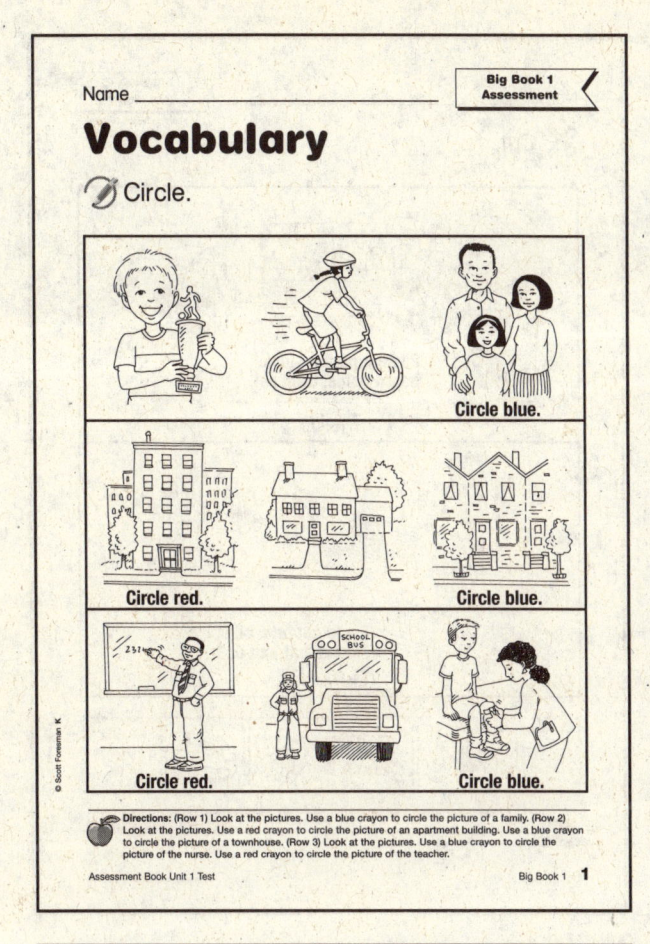

🅞 Circle.

Row 1: (boy with trophy) | (child on bike) | (family) **Circle blue.**

Row 2: (apartment building) **Circle red.** | (house) | (townhouse) **Circle blue.**

Row 3: (teacher at chalkboard) **Circle red.** | (school bus) | (nurse with child) **Circle blue.**

Directions: (Row 1) Look at the pictures. Use a blue crayon to circle the picture of a family. (Row 2) Look at the pictures. Use a red crayon to circle the picture of an apartment building. Use a blue crayon to circle the picture of a townhouse. (Row 3) Look at the pictures. Use a red crayon to circle the picture of the nurse. Use a red crayon to circle the picture of the teacher.

Assessment Book Unit 1 Test — Big Book 1 — 1

Color.

Big Book 1 Assessment — Reading Social Studies — Use Illustrations

Top: Child colors the coat, scarf, sweater, snow pants, boots, snowflakes, and sled.

Bottom: Child colors the sun, flowers, T-shirt, shorts, sandals, picnic basket, and toy in dog's mouth.

Directions: (Top) Color the picture clues that tell you it is cold outside. (Bottom) Color the picture clues that tell you it is hot outside.

2 — Big Book 1 — Assessment Book Unit 1 Test

How are people alike and different?

✏️ Color.

Top: Child colors the soccer uniform, soccer ball, girl's pigtails, dance leotard, tutu, ballet shoes, and girl's ponytail.

Bottom: Child colors both uniforms, bike helmets, and bikes.

Directions: (Top) Look at the picture to see how these girls are different. Color the things that are different about the girls. (Bottom) Look at the picture to see how these boys are alike. Color the things that are alike about the boys.

Assessment Book Unit 1 Test — Big Book 1 — 3

How are people alike and different?

🅞 Circle. ✏️ Draw.

Child circles red the children pushing, circles blue the child intervening, and adds self to picture.

Directions: Use a red crayon to circle the children who are not following good rules for being in a line. Use a blue crayon to circle the child who is trying to help. Draw yourself in the picture. Share your picture with a partner to tell how the children are alike and different.

4 — Big Book 1 — Assessment Book Unit 1 Test

Assessment Book — Answer Key — 25

Vocabulary

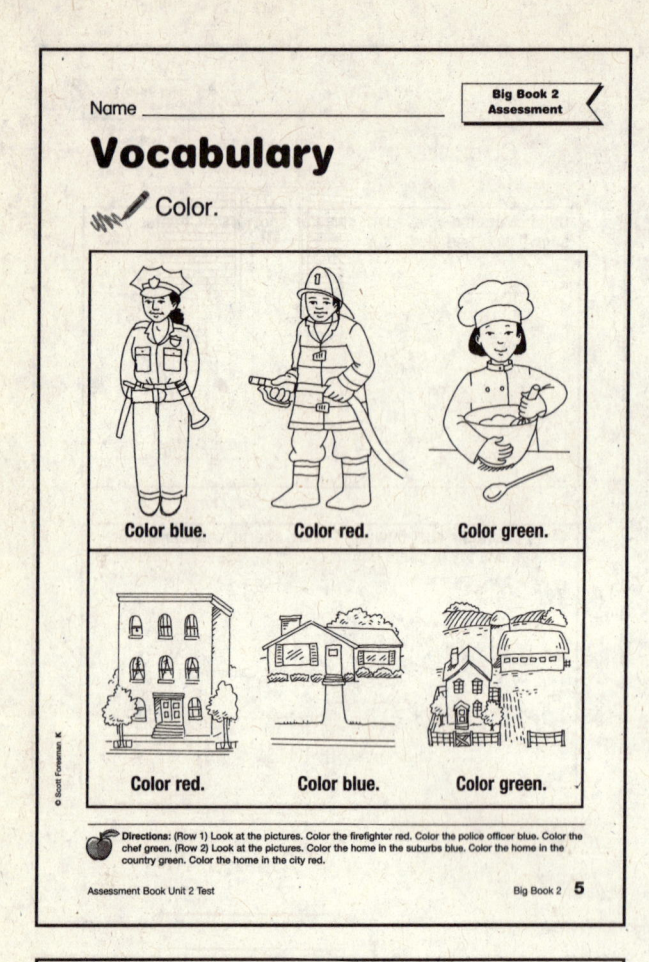

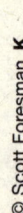

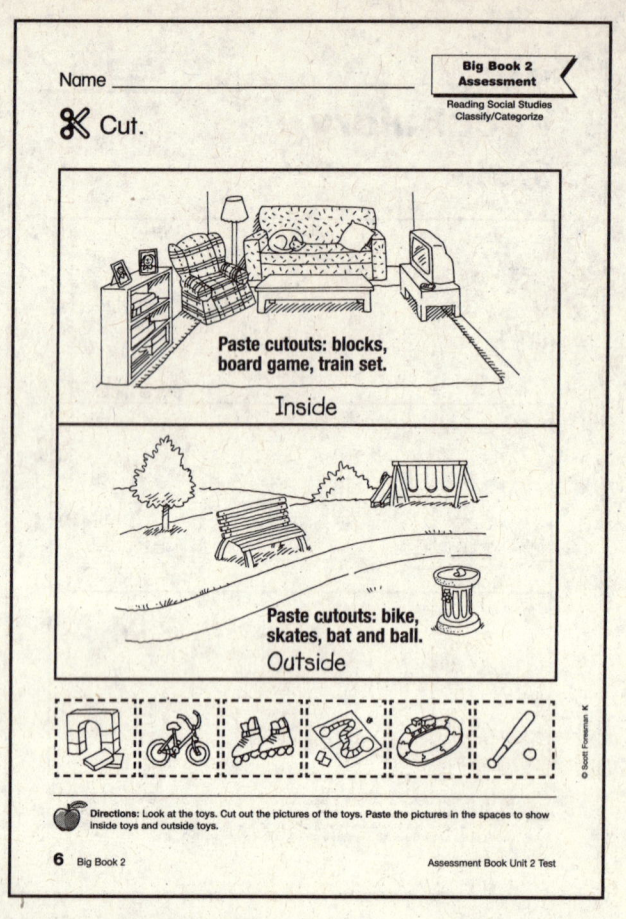

Color.

Row 1:
- Color blue. (police officer)
- Color red. (firefighter)
- Color green. (chef)

Row 2:
- Color red. (home in the city)
- Color blue. (home in the suburbs)
- Color green. (home in the country)

Directions: (Row 1) Look at the pictures. Color the firefighter red. Color the police officer blue. Color the chef green. (Row 2) Look at the pictures. Color the home in the suburbs blue. Color the home in the country green. Color the home in the city red.

Assessment Book Unit 2 Test — Big Book 2 5

Cut.

Reading Social Studies
Classify/Categorize

Paste cutouts: blocks, board game, train set.
Inside

Paste cutouts: bike, skates, bat and ball.
Outside

Directions: Look at the toys. Cut out the pictures of the toys. Paste the pictures in the spaces to show inside toys and outside toys.

6 Big Book 2 — Assessment Book Unit 2 Test

What is a community?

Circle. Circle signs: *stop* sign, *walk* sign, *arrows*, *wet paint*, *pedestrian crossing*, *bus stop*, *school*.

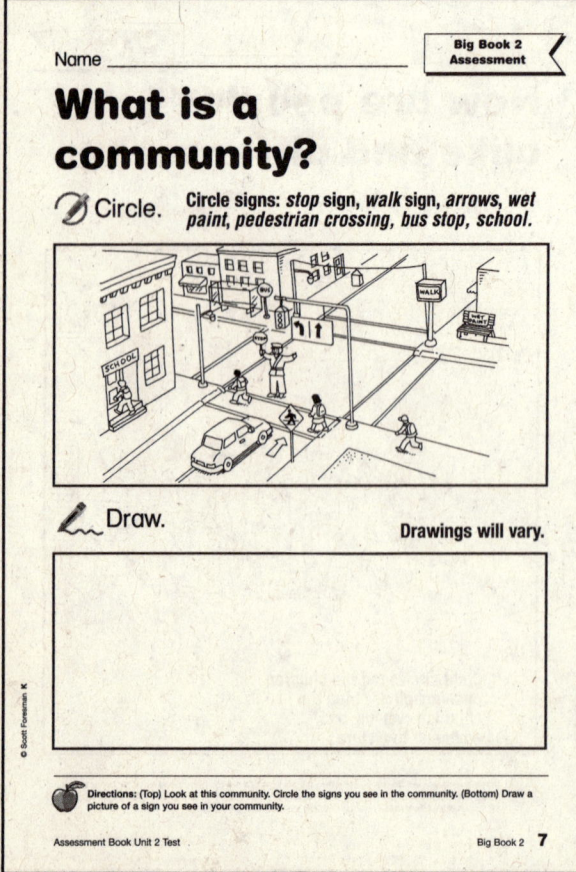

Draw. Drawings will vary.

Directions: (Top) Look at this community. Circle the signs you see in the community. (Bottom) Draw a picture of a sign you see in your community.

Assessment Book Unit 2 Test — Big Book 2 7

What is a community?

Circle.

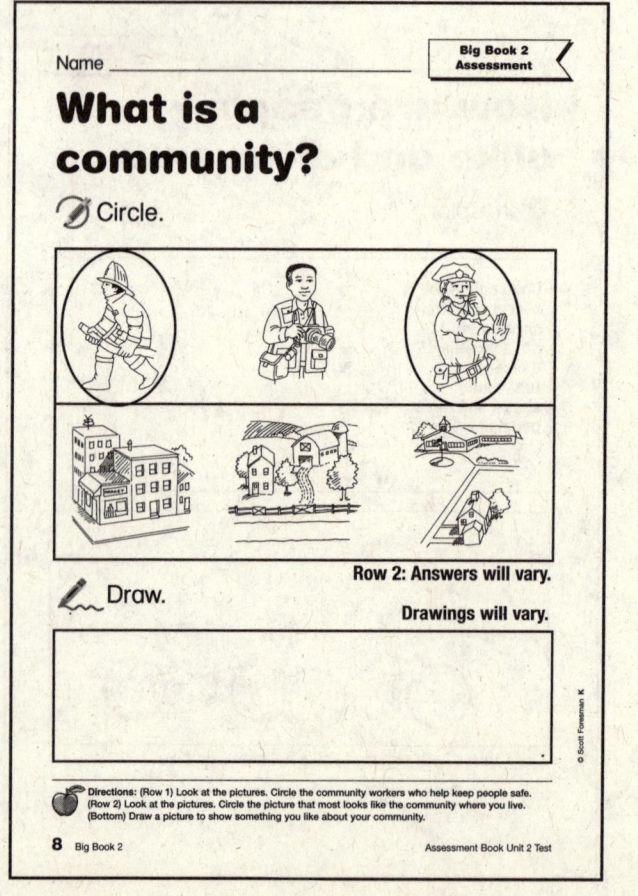

Row 2: Answers will vary.

Draw. Drawings will vary.

Directions: (Row 1) Look at the pictures. Circle the community workers who help keep people safe. (Row 2) Look at the pictures. Circle the picture that most looks like the community where you live. (Bottom) Draw a picture to show something you like about your community.

8 Big Book 2 — Assessment Book Unit 2 Test

---

26 Answer Key — Assessment Book

Vocabulary

Circle.

Circle blue.   Circle red.   Circle green.

Circle the food red, the clothing blue, and the shelter green.

Directions: (Top) Look at the pictures. Use a red crayon to circle the firefighter. Use a blue crayon to circle the chef. Use a green crayon to circle the photographer. (Bottom) Look at the picture. Use a red crayon to circle the food. Use a blue crayon to circle the clothing. Use a green crayon to circle the shelter.

Assessment Book Unit 3 Test — Big Book 3 — 9

Color. Color the girl's clothing, bike, address, and water from can.

Color the girl's clothing, bike, address, and water from hose.

Directions: Look at the two pictures. Think about how the pictures are alike and different. Color the things that are alike.

10 Big Book 3 — Assessment Book Unit 3 Test

What kinds of work do people do?

Color. Color the grocer, the mail carrier, the ambulance attendant, and the police officer.

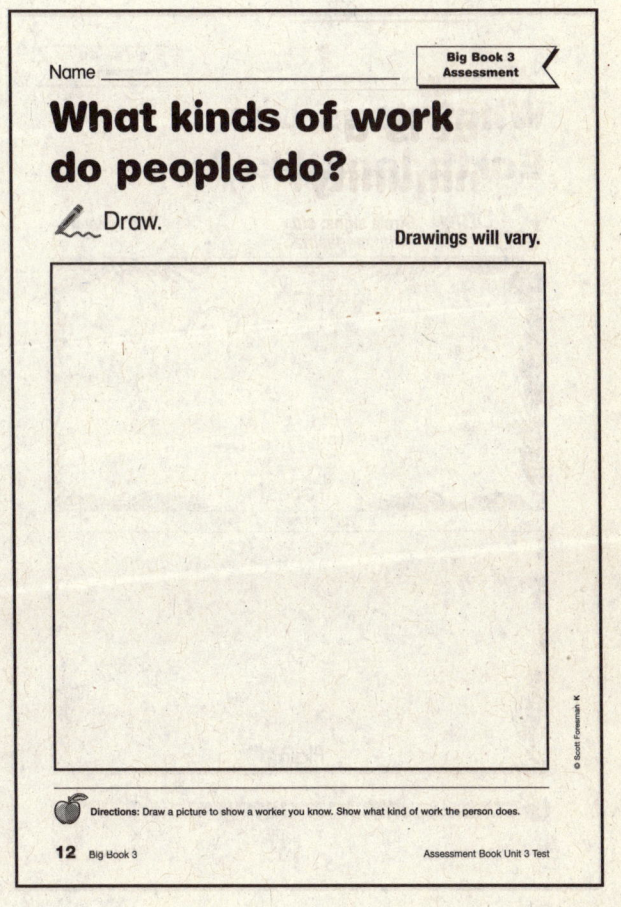

Directions: Look at the picture. Color the workers in the picture.

Assessment Book Unit 3 Test — Big Book 3 — 11

What kinds of work do people do?

Draw.

Drawings will vary.

Directions: Draw a picture to show a worker you know. Show what kind of work the person does.

12 Big Book 3 — Assessment Book Unit 3 Test

Assessment Book — Answer Key — 27

Vocabulary

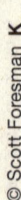

Circle.

Circle blue. Circle red. Circle green.

Circle green. Circle red. Circle blue.

Directions: (Top) Look at the pictures. Use a green crayon to circle the summer picture. Use a blue crayon to circle the winter picture. Use a red crayon to circle the fall picture. (Bottom) Look at the pictures. Use a green crayon to circle the forest picture. Use a blue crayon to circle the plains picture. Use a red crayon to circle the mountain picture.

Assessment Book Unit 4 Test — Big Book 4 — 13

Draw. Color.

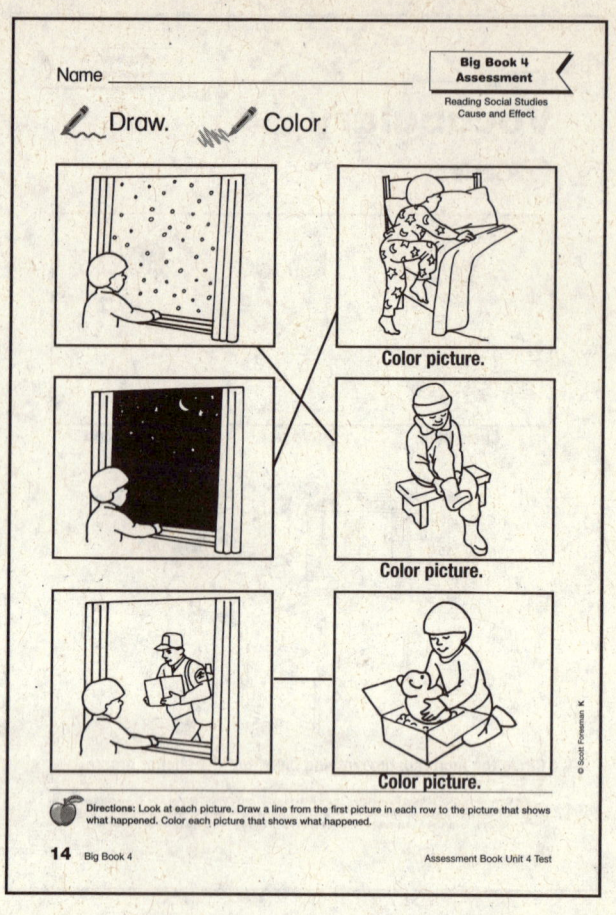

Color picture.
Color picture.
Color picture.

Directions: Look at each picture. Draw a line from the first picture in each row to the picture that shows what happened. Color each picture that shows what happened.

14 Big Book 4 — Assessment Book Unit 4 Test

Reading Social Studies
Cause and Effect

What does our Earth look like?

Draw. Drawings will vary.

Forest

Plain

Directions: (Top) Draw a picture to show a forest and an animal that might live there. (Bottom) Draw a picture to show a plain and an animal that might live there.

Assessment Book Unit 4 Test — Big Book 4 — 15

What does our Earth look like?

Draw. Drawings will vary.

Mountain

Ocean

Directions: (Top) Draw a picture to show a mountain and an animal that might live there. (Bottom) Draw a picture to show an ocean and an animal that might live there.

16 Big Book 4 — Assessment Book Unit 4 Test

Vocabulary

Circle.

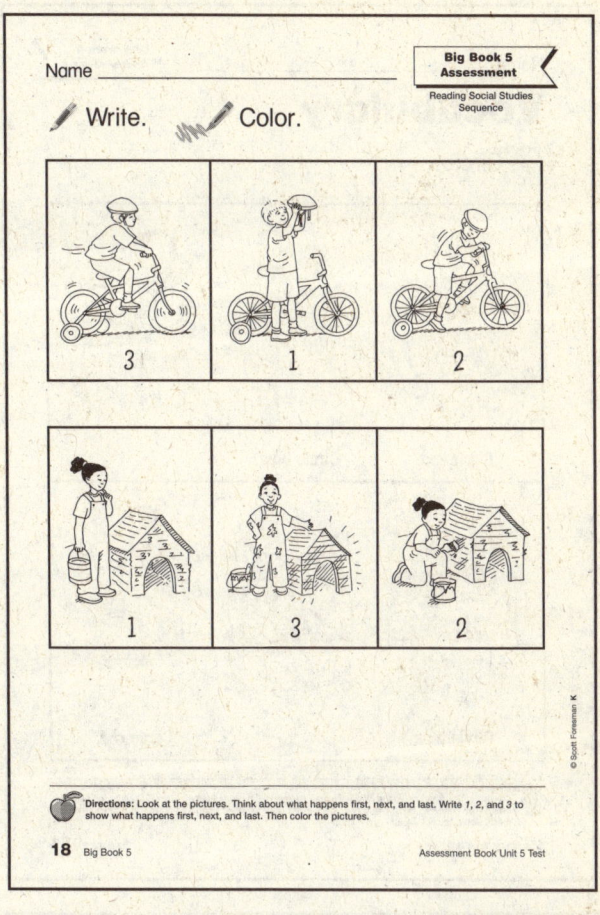

Directions: (Row 1) Look at the pictures. Use a blue crayon to circle the Statue of Liberty. Use a red crayon to circle the American flag. (Row 2) Look at the pictures. Use a blue crayon to circle Pocahontas. Use a red crayon to circle George Washington. (Row 3) Look at the pictures. Use a blue crayon to circle the train. Use a red crayon to circle the covered wagon.

Assessment Book Unit 5 Test — Big Book 5 17

Write. Color.

Reading Social Studies
Sequence

Row 1: 3, 1, 2
Row 2: 1, 3, 2

Directions: Look at the pictures. Think about what happens first, next, and last. Write 1, 2, and 3 to show what happens first, next, and last. Then color the pictures.

Big Book 5 — Assessment Book Unit 5 Test 18

How has our country changed?

Circle. Color.

Row 1: Now | (Then) circled ; (Now) circled | Then
Row 2: Now | (Then) circled ; (Now) circled | Then

Directions: Look at the pictures. Circle *Now* if the picture shows what our country is like today. Circle *Then* if the picture shows what our country was like long ago. Color the pictures.

Assessment Book Unit 5 Test — Big Book 5 19

How has our country changed?

Circle. Color.

Row 1: (Now) circled | Then ; Now | (Then) circled
Row 2: Now | (Then) circled ; (Now) circled | Then

Directions: Look at the pictures. Circle *Now* if the picture shows what our country is like today. Circle *Then* if the picture shows what our country was like long ago. Color the pictures.

Big Book 5 — Assessment Book Unit 5 Test 20

Vocabulary

Circle.

- Circle red.
- Circle blue.
- Circle blue.
- Circle red.

Directions: (Row 1) Look at the pictures. Use a blue crayon to circle one reason a family might celebrate. Use a red crayon to circle one way a family might play together. (Row 2) Look at the pictures. Use a blue crayon to circle one way a family might work together. Use a red crayon to circle something made with a family recipe.

Assessment Book Unit 6 Test — Big Book 6 21

Draw.

Reading Social Studies — Recall and Retell

Drawings will vary.

Directions: Think about an activity the class has done together. Draw a picture to recall the activity. Use your picture to retell the activity to the class.

22 Big Book 6 — Assessment Book Unit 6 Test

What is special about families?

Color.

Families work together.

Draw. Drawings will vary.

My family works together.

Directions: (Top) Color the picture of the family working together. (Bottom) Draw a picture to show a way your family works together. Then tell how the family pictures are alike and different.

Assessment Book Unit 6 Test — Big Book 6 23

What is special about families?

Color.

Families have fun together.

Draw Drawings will vary.

My family has fun together.

Directions: (Top) Color the picture of the family having fun together. (Bottom) Draw a picture to show a way your family has fun together. Then tell how the family pictures are alike and different.

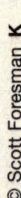

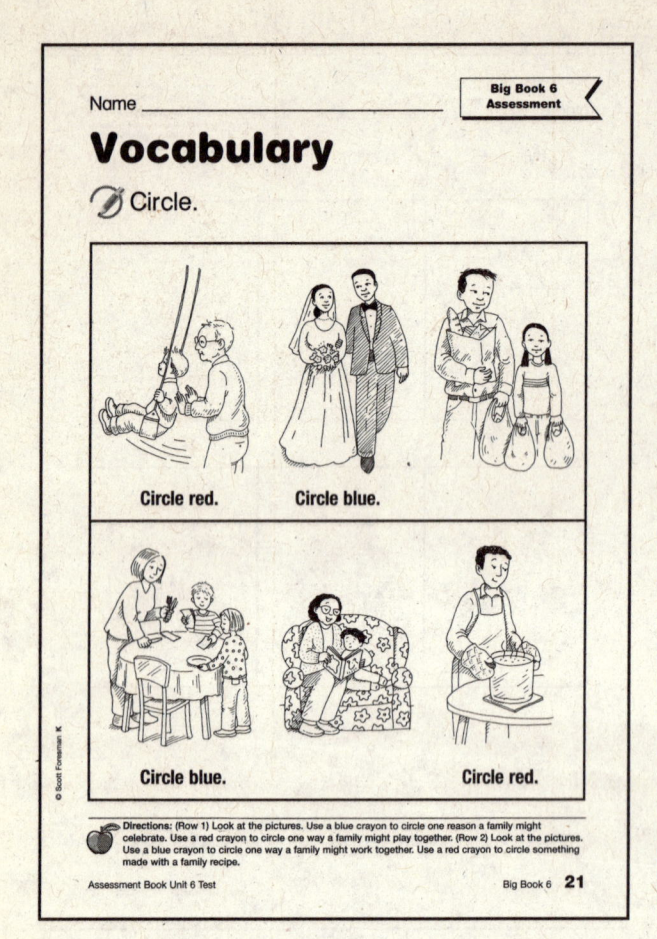

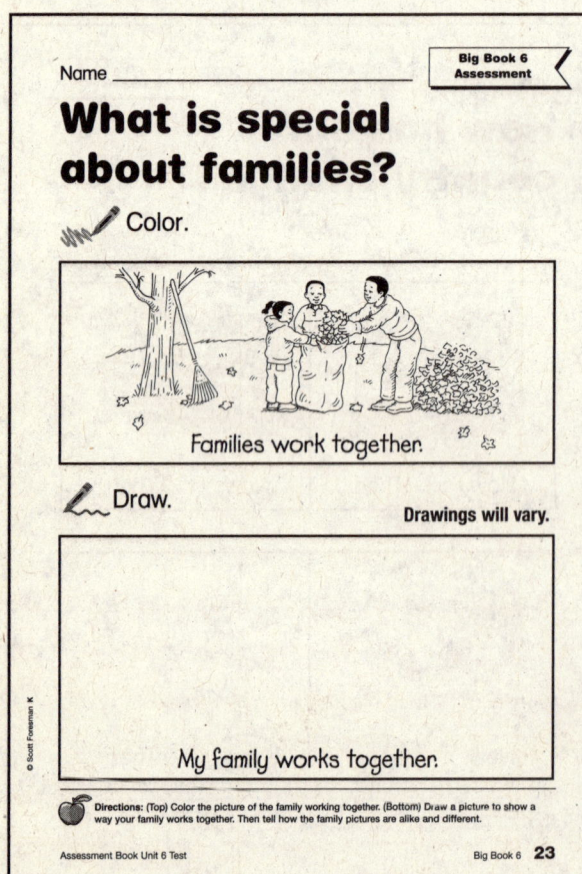

24 Big Book 6 — Assessment Book Unit 6 Test

---

30 Answer Key — Assessment Book

NOTES

NOTES

NOTES

NOTES

NOTES

NOTES

NOTES

NOTES

NOTES

NOTES